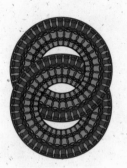

# KAZIMIERZ SQUARE

# Kazimierz Square

POEMS
## Karen Chase

CavanKerry ◊ Press LTD.

FORT LEE, NEW JERSEY

Library of Congress Cataloging-in-Publication Data

Chase, Karen
    Kazimierz Square / Karen Chase.
        p. cm.
    ISBN 0-9678856-0-4
        I. Title.

PS3553.H33464 K39 2000
811'.54—dc21                                                    00-029502

Cover art, detail from Barnum and Bailey poster, 1908,
courtesy Circus World Museum, Baraboo, Wisconsin

Lines from Sappho (page xiii) translated by Mary Barnard

Cover and text design by Charles Casey Martin

FIRST EDITION

IN MEMORY OF MY MOTHER

Lil Block

# CONTENTS

## THREE

## FOUR

# ACKNOWLEDGMENTS

Thanks to the editors of the publications in which these poems, some in slightly different versions, first appeared.

*The American Voice*: "The Swim," "At the Hospital," "Before She Died"
*Another Chicago Magazine (ACM)*: "Kazimierz Square"
*The Bad Henry Review*: "Rudimentary," "Southern Visit"
*The Berkshire Review*: "Sunday Afternoon Food"
*Buffalo Spree*: "Steam"
*Caliban*: "What You Can't See"
*Chiron Review*: "Abandoning Sadness"
*Exquisite Corpse*: "The A B C of What I've Been Called," "Last night on the 40th-floor balcony," "This Is What It's Like Going to a Language Poetry Poetry Reading"
*The Gettysburg Review*: "Circus in Lublin, 1942"
*Hawaii Review*: "Jimmy Keenan and I took off"
*The Louisville Review*: "There Are No Metaphors Tonight"
*The Nebraska Review*: "Beach Painting"
*The New Republic*: "Fever"
*The New Yorker*: "Venison"
*Poetry Ireland*: "Fishing the Wrecks"
*Puerto del Sol*: "Why Anything" (originally titled "Ending")
*The Seattle Review*: "The Krakow Fleamarket"
*Shenandoah*: "The Beach," "Gouldsboro"
*Willow Springs*: "Aspects of Luck"
*The Yale Review*: "Winter in Provincetown"

*Yellow Silk*: "This Can Happen When You're Married," "Somewhat a
        Visitor," "Stubborn sheets," "My eyes stop on your arms"
        (originally titled "My House")

"Venison" also appears in *The Norton Introduction to Literature* (7th
edition), *The Norton Introduction to Poetry* (7th edition) (W.W. Norton,
1998), and *Hungry For You* (Chatto and Windus, 1997).

"Iceland" also appears in *Under One Roof* (Mad River Press, 1992).

"What You Can't See" also appears in *The Jazz Poetry Anthology, The
Second Set* (University of Indiana Press, 1996).

"This Can Happen When You're Married" also appears in *Yellow Silk,
Erotic Arts and Letters* (Crown Publishers, 1990).

"This Is What It's Like Going to a Language Poetry Poetry Reading"
also appears in *Thus Spake The Corpse: An Exquisite Corpse Reader,
1988–1998*, Volume I, (Black Sparrow Press,1999).

I thank The Rockefeller Foundation for a stay at the Bellagio Center,
where the title poem "Kazimierz Square" was completed.

# FOREWORD

Painting and photography are things Karen Chase does well; so are fishing and cooking. I never met anyone quite so vividly and rewardingly at home with putting together a meal.

About some poets these data might seem irrelevant: here, they are of a piece with the poetry, and indeed prepare a reader as nearly as anything can for a poetic voice of such earthy directness, on the one hand, and on the other of such visionary power. Of literary antecedents I see no clue at all. John Donne would acknowledge the bedroom scenes, Seamus Heaney the settings of "Gouldsboro"—

> The clammer hauls
> his boat over the stones

—and "Rudimentary" ("Spuds / taste of the ground / beneath // So I like words / how they grab hold / of the earth / with their underground / stock"), as he would the fascination with those of Eastern Europe. An actual tour through Poland, as I understand, culminated in the demonic astonishments of "Kazimierz Square," the long poem that gives this collection its title. Strong stuff it undoubtedly is—being just as undoubtedly an instance of the poet in the grip of the poem, rather than the other way round. As one whose own work falls in the category of the "cooked," I have a natural admiration for the raw power of its demonic imagery. But that raw power ought not to mislead a reader as to the distinctive cadence of the language itself. Karen Chase's gift for turning a phrase, her ear for the throaty music to be found in the lower registers of English speech, are uniquely hers, to be listened for with pleasure.

*—Amy Clampitt*

If you are squeamish
Don't prod the
beach rubble

—Sappho

# ◆ONE◆

# Venison

Paul set the bags down, told how they had split
the deer apart, the ease of peeling it
simpler than skinning a fruit, how the buck
lay on the worktable, how they sawed
an anklebone off, the smell not rank.
The sun slipped into night.

*Where are you* I wondered as I grubbed
through cupboards for noodles at least.
Then came venison new with blood,
stray hair from the animal's fur.
Excited, we cooked the meat.

Later, I dreamt against your human chest,
you cloaked me in your large arms, then
went for me the way you squander food sometimes.
By then, I was eating limbs in my sleep, somewhere
in the snow alone, survivor of a downed plane,
picking at the freshly dead. Whistles
of a far off flute—legs, gristle, juice.
I cracked an elbow against a rock, awoke.
Throughout the night, we consumed and consumed.

# Circus in Lublin, 1942

There was no music,
no one played the cimbalom.
Ladies dressed in largesized brassieres cheered
Yablo as he poured himself into a glass.
In formation, ducklings waddled around him, belching.
An odor of soup filled the tent.

Trained geese crooned to Yablo in Hungarian,
rugsellers told tales to noblemen,
lions turned puny.
A stench hung over all Lublin.
There were those who complained.

A bear walked across the stage in tears.
Flowers cracked open the floorboards,
grew before the crowd.
Fragrant roses, painted daisies, yellow iris.
Penguins marched out, placed ties around
the necks of plants.
Roseface, Daisyface, Irisface.
Against the upper reaches of the tent, parrots
fluttered 'til their feathers dropped.

Outdoors, from slagheaps, walls were built.
A great deal of crockery broke.
A fleshy woman sold mushrooms on the street.
Another, stray plums.

They placed tablecloths beneath their wares,
then newspaper, then the bowls of measly pears.
Men waited for word from anywhere.

# The Krakow Fleamarket

In a field of mud,
one man held up one shirt
for sale, all day
in the aimless rain.
Lines of people
stood by their wares.

"One tooth, one zloty.
Buy it for your mother.
Thread string
through the toothhole.

One shoe, two zlotys.
Next week find another.
Today, half your toes
will be covered."

A horse lived
by the fleamarket,
stayed inside.
For comfort,
he listened to radio static.

He had loved the woods,
loved to be out
among the hollyhocks
and long-bellied birds.

Afraid now of birds,
of the fleamarket,
he'd look at his hooves.

One day he heard
a miner was
rounding up animals
to paint.
Scared he'd get caught
in a painting,
he nailed his door shut.

A hunter with shoulders
hunched so high
his neck went,
patrolled the woods
to find animals
for his friend to paint.

To escape his eyes,
the long-bellied birds
rose from the ground.
The horse couldn't fly.

The coal miner never rose
to the level of ground.
With warm breath,
he'd squint at his palette
in the lightless mine,
paint what his hunter friend
said he'd seen.
From hearsay, he'd paint.

So the scared horse
remained inside,
the sellers of goods
stood in the rain.
A hoof, a tooth, a shoe
for sale, with a washed-out
notion of what money buys.

# Taking Turns Mourning

Years may pass and
the mourner feels
nothing, it's wrong
to call her a mourner
she's not sad
like the others
no missing happens
rarely a passing thought even
of the one who is
lost and gone then something
like seeing light
fulminate from an alleyway
and all at once begins her loss.

# Winter in Provincetown

On the dunes
in my dreams
there are parties
for the dead

The Saw Mill
The Hutch
The Merritt
I can't get there


•


My dead dog Mop got loose
I watched the moon go down


•


Fried, stuffed, stewed—
it's squid night in this one

stars are out

*calamari*—me drinking ink


•

•

Balloons
a seal dried on the beach
Sappho saying *squeamish*

Dark wine—the radio on loud
traces of our clam feast
My dead mother walking around—confetti—she's fine—
winter nights in Provincetown

# The A B C of What I've Been Called

Too bad the alphabet starts with A because
I've been called Asshole
Baby, Buddy, Bitch, and Babe
I've been called Cookie and Cunt but
Nothing for D or E
Plenty of times, I've been called Fuck
G for Girl and Gal
Honeybunny, Honey
Nothing for I, no J, but now for K
Karen, Karey (by a small niece)
Kacey (by a former friend), Karina
Karen Sue Block (born that way)
Karen Chase (married at 20)
Karen Graubard (again at 40)
Karen Block Chase
Karen Chase Graubard
Cherna Sussel (Yiddish—as a drummer in a band)
L for Lovey and Lamb
Missy, Miz, Mrs., Ma'am
Mama, Mommy, Mom, Ma
Mistress Karen (by Roosevelt Tom)
Mademoiselle (in my youth), Madame (last month)
No N's
No O's
P for Poochie, Pal, and Pussycat
No Q's
No R's
For S, Sugarina and Shit

Sugartits and Sis
T, U, V
W for Whore
X, Y, Zenas Block's daughter.

# Fever

The arsonist with close-cropped hair
meandering down the neck of whitewashed air,
clad in wet leaves and plaid bathrobe,
flammable nightshirt underneath.

Tree limbs turned watery,
trunks red gray in the way far away,
smoke choked the scene, every rung shook.

I was 10, rapped with polio and the night
rose from the yard like a large bird.

The ambulance blare cleaved
the air like meat under a knife.
From then on, everything was before or after like war.

Flames climbed through my kindling feet,
seeped down my arms
hot abdomen
chest
about-to-be-developed breasts.

Mouth, tongue, palate parched,
no water could appease my need to drink.
*Where are my feet?*

In the aftermath, I threw dead shoes of no use in a heap,
picked up a brush, a lure.

Cubes, nudes,
green paintings afloat in seedy forests but lush,
cool fish of all types.
I moved.

# Last night on the 40th-floor balcony,

2 little girls and I stood
joking. Rivers on both sides,
the Statue of Liberty on the right.

The smaller wore an aqua shirt,
the larger, a red one. I lifted the
larger up, put her down, thought,
*in dreams you can do this*, lifted
her again, threw her over the railing.

She flew down slowly, her length grew,
her width widened, her little body now
a puppet 3 stories high, legs billowing
out, aqua arms wings of a birdgirl.
She landed in a heap on the ground.
Then I heaved the other one over the railing.

# Come to Bed

1.

My eyes stop on your arms
your thin torso.
Every object shivers
every object charms.

As you bend to turn out the lamp
I see your red underwear inch
past the waist of your pants.

Let's banish the words
books and brains, vanish!
I love the hair on your legs.
Come, I whisper, to bed.

You've never seen the inside
of my house, you're in my bed
now, your tongue's in my mouth.

2.

I've been intrigued with the way you run
your fingers over your lips,
back and forth as if to learn their shape,
"to ease them," you say.

I wonder what you notice about me.

I know you'd love my thighs,
their unexpected width.
They are wide.

After my fingers have kissed your lips
and my lips have fingered your ears and eyes,
your mouth, your lips, your tongue,
everything—goes straight for my thighs.

3.

Stubborn sheets,
quilts heaped,
our heads belong
on jumbled pillows,
our mouths
within kissing
distance

My fingers run
over your lips,
you open my mouth
with yours

One hand
smoothes
my hair,
the other
explores

4.

Here I am again content
on your couch, dogs though
begin to bark.

Out the window, unruly leaves
break from the trees, but
you're here, brushing my cheek.

Your dogs, you say,
are ready for love.
You're my doctor
no harm will come.

Raucous dogs ready at the door
distinct from your quiet roar.

I've dreamt this dream you know
you slide me down the couch
it's storming out, you turn me
over, you will take care.

You draw my face with your hands
make my back feel okay
you will watch, simply watch,
you say.

5.

You draw stories with old characters,
a mystery to me.
I have written, thought, had my day.

You're lying on your back,
not quite in the mood, you say.

Both weary, we rest,
a word here and there,
the sheets back and forth,
a current makes its persistent way.

I feel you start to harden against me,
my flesh goes toward you,
pink turns red bright,
my breasts say *mouth, mouth* they say
to your lips tonight.

## 6. *Sunrise*

Your dawn caress dispels
the still deep dark.
A pastel haze.
"But I'm asleep" I say.
You lick my dreams with lazy eyes
spread my thighs
paint me with your tongue
slide inside.
I'm wet, I'm soft, I'm sleepy.
I'm on my side.

We barely move
as we three rise.

7.

Something bad has happened,
I don't know.

I've been walking in the snow where
I used to live, in a wind.

All I want is to sleep, shut my eyes,
not say a thing.

I throw off my clothes,
turn to the wall.

You come to bed too.
My flesh has forgotten itself,
I am gone.
Then you turn me toward you.

# ◆TWO◆

# The Evening

In Arezzo there's no breeze.
We pass the piazza slowly
ignore the heat. Up we meander
up the streets.
We close the door to our room
open windows that face a lawn.

Boys at play sound
from a nearby roof
marigolds fill our room.

When we met
I barely noticed your hair.
Now I see its graying
I see your color.

Striped dusk creams the night
muted streets outside.
Maybe I love you I don't know
we hold down the dawn now.

# Somewhat a Visitor

I think of us in towns I don't know, Arezzo
at siesta or the outskirts of Memphis,
the pots of marigolds are gone now, no corny songs
in the car.

Stirred last night from a leaden sleep, I wished
I could memorize your flesh, take it in
like a Shakespeare sonnet that barely would leave.

I think how your thighs would stretch out for me
to rest on like a small spent animal after a long feed.
Then once more you'd swarm above me, somewhat a visitor.
I wonder how your arms feel beneath your shirt,
your willful lengthy legs as guides,
your talkless tongue waking my hesitant breath.

Will you know my skin after the first
breezefilled dare, after the indelible
darkfold marks of lovemaking?

Separated by hours of sleep, we might wake
to a climate we can't leave, walk
outside to the iris bed to weed and weed.

# Southern Visit

I'm a northerner on an extra chair.
Some girl in her 4th month
is starting to show shape, her mother's
traveling north with a suitcase of oysters.
They chew on gristle, pick bones so clean
they're white. Dinner takes a long time.

If I lived here, I'd stay in bed late,
sit at breakfast with my mother and sister,
take turns telling nightmares like they were stories.
We'd each have three cups of coffee, share a plate
of doughnuts. So what if we'd hear a car lurch out front.

I'd meander downtown, eavesdrop on the bar sounds.
I'd watch men play dominoes outside a store, wonder
who the floral offering on the pickup is for.
I'd throw back my shoulders, be aware of my ass,
pout the right amount. I'd notice a man
who'd never been in town before,
notice his knife as he peels a pear.

Marking the drive with which he strips that pear,
I'd catch sight of a bed with pink covers
through a window, look around
for an exit and a souvenir.

# Aspects of Luck

When a small
woman, such as
me, catches a large
fish, such as a 20
lb. salmon,
it is luck.

I am short, it bit, it
was luck, the fish was
big. I fought, it
fought, I felt big, I
drove quick
to Poulsbo to

have it smoked.
I have thought of good
fortune and luck, good
fortune and skill, and skill
and luck, but

luck it was and lucky too,
*because* I am short,
it was big,
we fought and now,
it is smoked.

Now that I've written
"Aspects of Luck," it's

next to the picture of me and
the fish, the question comes up of
which is worth more—god knows.

# Fishing the Wrecks

Six A.M. at Sheffield Arms,
the fishermen's pub by the car park,
our skipper Larry Ryan
orders a grease-out—
beans, eggs, and a slab of bacon that looks like ham.

"Eat," says Larry
"We'll be out for 8 or 10 hours."
The waves are green in the Channel, a drizzle.
On shore are white humps of chalk.
Seven Sisters, the hills are called,
to the left, that cliff is Beachy Head. And behind,
the town of Battle where the Battle of Hastings was fought.

Larry Ryan's radio is playing Verdi's *Requiem*.
A fisherman puts live bait on his line,
"live bite," he calls it. On comes *Ode to Joy*.
The fishermen are discussing
this particular rendition,
hauling in sea bass,
I am concentrating on my line.
"Virginia Woolf's house is right off
Lewes-Newhaven Road," someone says,
baits his hook, dirty jokes over the shortwave mix with Berlioz.

We are fishing above torpedoed wrecks,
200 boats sunk by Germans in a 10-mile radius.

Now they're talking about Dunkirk.
I did not catch a fish.

"Do the wrecks have names?" I ask.
"Yes"—Larry's reply.
"What do you call them?"
"Nothing—no-one's business where I fish.
Hold this big bass up, I'll take your picture.
You're not a real fisherman until you lie."

# Vowels

"I may lose my sight," you told my husband
as you watched the Celtics game in the dark bar.
My old doctor, we don't see each other anymore.

We have no room now where we notice the light,
no window to look at when
we look away, there's no way
to tell you I love how you say *beautiful*
the *i* like a long *e*.
I've been thinking of vowels lately.

There are trees all colors of green this morning,
there's rain, I hear the *e*'s and see the greens—
what if you couldn't see? I'm listening
to sweet Al Green sing his vowels now, how
they stretch on *huuuuuuuuuuuuhhhh*

# Why Anything

The body remembers what the mind forgets.
I looked at your face last night, both of us unconsummate.
My cheeks knew the glaze of your palms' press,
my mouth would not erase the gaze of yours,
how we'd map together our lips, pore by pore.
Whatever it was, I did dirty work just to be near,
bent forward, backward, over the bed,
stooped so you could fatten on me.
My body unblushing went wanting more.
Your face at times was a disk with no inside,
eyes, mouth, chin
laminated together, starting to undo.
Nothing changed on this planet
the way your eyes did.
They got like brass, sunk away.
My arms ache, my neck forgets which way to turn.
My breasts don't know why anything.

# Iceland

You stand there north
and cold in the sea
hissing fire.
On a bare table
you set out a feast of promises
hardly clothed at all.
I never looked so hard at nothing.

I walk back
through your black sands
gathering shadows
humming for comfort.
Struck by a lone flower
I live in it all I can.

# Steam

There are hints no matter when or where,
the earth throws off her force.
Like when a storm drops down
on the lake at home, sound seizes the air or
when my sister's belly grows, her baby moves.

Once the windshield wiper broke
as we drove across the coast of Iceland.
We couldn't tell the river from the road so
my husband, sons, and I drove the riverbed
as though it were a thoroughfare. Steam rose,
ice and heat blurred the snow. We knew from maps
a glacier was near, but our vision swam from us
in this morass. We stopped the car,
ran to the hot river, threw down our clothes and swam.

Now my son is a young man.
We've just been to a local resort where my son,
sweating in the steam room, leapt
to the pool. To the steam room I went, dropped
the sheet to the floor, stretched
across the wooden slats, sweating.
As if to copy him, I rose up, dashed
to the cold hotel pool, dove with no reserve.

## This Is What It's Like Going to a Language Poetry Poetry Reading.

For the first 30 seconds, you go over in your mind whether you're exhausted and that must be why you can't concentrate. You remember you're not tired.

For the second minute, you decide that concentrating will require a great deal of effort, but it's worth it. You tell yourself to muster all your prowess to understand the poem.

You give up.

For the next few minutes, you notice every detail of each person in the audience—their hair, their sweaters—you weigh whether they like sex, are they students? Et cetera.

This lasts only so long.

You get so bored, you think you will die.

The reader has just informed the audience that her next poem will take 25 minutes to read. You start to have trouble breathing.

a
a
a
the, the, the the
back

to
wit

hickory
and so James Fenimore

    Cooper

5
15
yes
and
adorn


You think of killing her. You think she's killing you. You think of so much murder, you're scared to go to your car in the dark.

# While Learning to Grow Trout

In the hatchery, billions of teeny trout—
browns, brookies, six bins of rainbows.
Zak scoops a curved one out, says,
"Get rid of them irregulars
before they start growing foodsize."

A shop near the fish farm sells dyed rabbits' feet.
I reach in my pocket for my old one,
now mainly bones, the fur worn off, then
buy a few new ones for friends.

Years it takes to rub luck from a foot—that's age
for you! It's not all sweating and graying
your way to the grave.
Paul and I drive through the Smokies,

pick up boiled peanuts and corn liquor
nearly too strong to drink. We discuss stresses
on fish—disease, floods, drought—worry
about a glutted market. We consider
the water flow per minute back home.

# What You Can't See

In the winter stadium, picturing
what you can't see, Leontyne
Price or Lena Horne, the night
the trumpet player died, people
picnicking on the lawn. For him,
his cohorts broke into some long Bach,
then some jazz, wanting songs
to reflect from the nearby lake.
The players played color tones,
saxophones could have grazed his skin.
Picture blues swinging off this empty stadium.

All night long, looking
out the train window
on the way to Birmingham,
watching I couldn't see what,
turned the light out, pulled
the bed down, watched
the whole state of Virginia in the dark.

It gets light.
I ask a trainman the name of a low
pink weed that grows by the track.
"Honey, we call them daffodils."
There's nothing universal here. Cows
are lounging now in what must be Georgia.
Trees that lost their names last night come
clean this morning, dirt red as blush.

# Abandoning Sadness

"Find another home," said the white woman
who fucked a black man then
didn't want the child who came.
"Find another home," she said, left

for the woods. It wasn't any stone
she left her on, but like a monument,
a flat one.
She came on it

with chirp and motor of baby,
with infant odor on her skin,
puke slung over her width.
She tightened the sling,

traipsed from the town green.
In these woods, slant trees
poled in place. From a far church,
bells clanged out of tune.

The dark girl wiggled
her baby length against her.
The woman sang Italian,
made nicknames up for sadness,
Tristina, Tezza.

She wanted a guide. Inside
these woods, she picked up

a handful of dirt. "Good-bye," she said,
flung nuts at her child. It was quick

back to her porch. She roasted
a hen, stuffed it with apricots.

# Gouldsboro

He clams the tides at night,
a light on his forehead.
Slosh of mud, effort
to pull each boot up, he works
and rakes the bay's empty mouth.

Listening in bed, how shell-like
the dark. Hum of wind spurs
this night, sounds of sea loosen here.
The clammer hauls
his boat over the stones.

# ◆ THREE ◆

# The Swim

Still she has her silent say.

I swam nude in a creek with my mother once,
we kept a distance.
Then she said how nice I looked. Sun

on her dark hair, wet curls on her neck,
she painted cadmium red canvases. My flesh

cushions my bones, when will we get over
her drawnout death? That creek has filled

with thawed snow, her lilies are beginning
to bloom, the sky now is begging for notice.

# A Walk

I stayed with my mother
when she was dying,
watched her limbs thin, wish
erased fear, I held
her invaded arms,

walked beaches
for birdbones,
fit together
parts of crabs, dropped
a boat board
I hauled along the sand.

The sea whitens bones,
moistens squid remains,
it hoards shards.
Feeding from the beach,
gulls fall toward clams.

# At the Hospital

Before the gardeners
turn up, the peony petals
fallen from yesterday's rain
litter the formal garden.

It's early morning as I walk
up and down each row—poppy row,
unplanted row, old iris,
some scrawny seedlings.

Yesterday, my first day
at work since my mother died,
I wanted to move in—pack my skirts,
shoes, leave my husband, my house.

Now, sitting on this stone bench,
tall yellow roses around me,
their odor caught in the wet
air, my bare feet on the lawn,
I am wearing my mother's old jacket.
Like never before, she's close.

# Jimmy Keenan and I took off

our shoes, walked
between tomato rows
got dirt on our feet.
So what
about planes overhead
1945
a war was far away.

For the first time
I noticed that beets grew
and peas on a vine.

Jimmy and I played
through the afternoon
then went to the roofs
by the lake
emptied our pockets
and jumped down.

Buttercups filled the fields.
I picked some for my mother
so she'd feel better
held them under my chin
to prove I liked butter.

It must have gotten late.
Far away the war was on
lights were turned low.

# Before She Died

When I look at the sky now, I look at it for you.
As if with enough attention, I could take it in for you.

With all the leaves gone almost from
the trees, I did not walk briskly through the field.

Late today with my dog Wool, I lay down in the upper field,
he panting and aged, me looking at the blue. Leaning

on him, I wondered how finite these lustered days seem
to you. A stand of hemlock across the lake catches

my eye. It will take a long time to know how it is
for you. Like a dog's lifetime—long—multiplied by sevens.

# There Are No Metaphors Tonight

The dry spider hinged to the ceiling is
a spider; the lamp, a lamp.

I try to lasso
the chair with my mind's rope, or the

map. Outside, the wind dutifully
blows night into place.

# The Beach

Always woken by thoughts of bodies
I never sleep late—my mother's bony
toes, long feet.

At the beach now, I'm stretched level
to the horizon, mold my privates
into cold sand, deeper than my face.

My knees bend into the beach,
my elbows cove into the sand.
The sand is hands underneath,

compass grass and rubble near my feet.
I don't care about my mother's hands—
geese are cranking away—
mix of my body and body of beach.

Her hold was cold when she was alive.
The sharp angles her elbows made,
her wide mute face.

# This Can Happen When You're Married

You find blue sheets the color of sky with
the feel of summer, they smell like clothes
drying on the line when you were small.
They feel unusual on your skin; you and your
husband sleep on them.

You find thick white towels that absorb
water. When you come from the bath, you are
cold for a moment, you think of snow for a moment,
you wrap yourself in a towel, dry off the water.

Now, you unpack your silver, after years, polish it,
set it in red quilted drawers your mother
lined for you when you were young.

You and your husband are in bed. The windows are open.
There is a smell from the lawn. It's dark and late. You
and your husband are in the sheets. He is like a horse.
You are like grass he is grazing, you are his field. Or
he's a cow in a barn, licking his calf. It's raining out.

He gets up, walks to the other room. You listen
for his step, his breath. It is late. For moments
before you sleep, you hear him singing.

He comes to bed. He touches your face. He touches
your chin and lips. Later, he tells you this. He puts

his head on your breast. You are dreaming of Rousseau now, paintings of girls and deserts and lions.

# Beach Painting

During the painting, a man looks up the dunes,
blue bathing trunks, distinct in shape
not in color from the sea. A woman curls
on a blanket, her legs folded at the knee,
light falling on her rear.
A bather has left the painting, walked down the beach,
left his chair.

Others walk off into that same thick sea
with its here and now blues. They proceed
out too far, so it's hard to know
what they ever thought. Out of the frame,
a balding man hugs at the sand.
Day closes down and the painting ends.
The figures still on the canvas want to go home.
Wind picks up on Commercial Street.

*—for Fran Dropkin*

# Sunday Afternoon Food

The rain lays music
on all things, the horn closes
on words like   Food   Ape

Coo.  I'm lying on the floor,
an orange hibiscus just fell
from the plant by the sliding
glass door.

Sunday afternoon
and the rain

is flooding the yard. I say
to Paul, "This has to be
one of the best days—
nothing's wrong.

No, not that—whatever's
wrong though, is so old
by now." Paul's watching
the Patriots play, we've been

back to bed, I listened to a
tape of foghorns and John
Cage say   Coo   Ice   Food
Ape   Do.  Got so bored. Talked

to my ex-husband on the phone.
Tried to work, then
opened some wine. Sounds inch up
piecemeal almost to the point

of sense—but
the flooded lawn.
"Bake. Bake. Bake."
A fleet of geese swim by. What

I wonder, are
the peepers dreaming, what
are the loons from Maine scheming,
what is screeching right now
in Chesapeake Bay?

All along the eastern seaboard
maritime is turning to song. Sunday
afternoon

only the urbaned
and determined
accomplish anything
on a day this long.

I was once so
lonesome watching the rain
out my window,
nothing was clear outdoors.

"The rain," I thought,
"and the wet Nile are the same."

The tide
going out off the Cedar Island Bridge,
a drainage pipe—
boys fishing for eels.

A lighthouse,
my mother and I standing by it,
she was dark and beautiful, I
don't know

if I remember it.
I do recall puddles on Columbus
Avenue when my boys were small.

And a ferry in
Mexico with peppers and fruit,
the ache of food.

I wouldn't mind living right now
inside the rain
coming down and down,
in fact I'm there now.
How stanzas are like rooms,
how long everything takes.

# Rudimentary

I like the taste
of root crops

Spuds
taste of the ground
beneath

So I like words
how they grab hold
of the earth
with their underground
stock

I like to uproot them
wet their offshoots
give them a new spot
to stretch

I like to watch
them creep
over the ground

# ◆FOUR◆

# Kazimierz Square

Past the long wood table, set with herring
and schnapps, I walk through the schul
to the women's back room. Up and down
men dahven, humming insect sound. Leaderless
they scuffle and pray. Through the lace-draped
window, I watch, take out my pen.
A beaver-hatted man swirls, spins, spots me
through the lace. Wigged women surround me,
try to pull my pen away.
"Here you do nothing but pray."
I leave the sanctuary. On a park bench, I touch my pen.

I head straight for Kazimierz Square.
"Please, officer, let me near the music."
A choir of shy Bulgarians en route for days
to pray before *The Black Madonna* stop.
Violas groan.
"No breadbasket here," they hum,
reach their hands in their pockets,
eye the axes in the truck, scared
to call notice to their voices and arms.

The viola players' fingers swell to the size
of corn ears, the drummer's right leg has lost
all flesh, turned to muscle from nights
of pedaling the bass. His leg powers
out a boom, shakes the rooms in nearby buildings

whose fronts are falling.
The concert in Kazimierz begins to move, it
is 1942. A band of children push a piano
around the Square, outlining its perimeter.

The bass drum enlarges its beat, so there's no
time in between. The piano player continues his song
out of tune. Curly-haired viola players tune
to the sour piano. A birdbone gets caught in my throat.
My choke adds to the dissonance.

A teenage couple hot with love of God, hike on
to church. Filmy choir sounds hover above the Square,
red-winged blackbirds swoop to the ground.
From a tower, a trumpeter's notes are cut short
to mark the moment he was shot.

A breeze blows sneeze gas through the cracks,
hunger butter trailing from a truck lures me farther,
*soft yellow pierogi dough* the truckdriver whistles,
I can't tell sound from smell,
piled-up turnips about to rust.

Brown-furred wild boar single file enter the Square,
their mobile snouts made live by the smell.
In their stomachs—canary feet, crawling meat, lettuce.
I join the hog march, fall to the ground.
Everything around is tuneless, the rain
is starting to fall and it is not fresh.
The wind comes up, blows like it's caught in a box,

sends the rain sideways,
carries stink into everyone's nose.
All my being knows now is needing food,
my skin grows fur, my eyes turn marble.
So what if they fall out.
Anything for food once the snout is alive.

The black night with rain beating,
a woman in a hog-drawn carriage has orange
poppies in her hand. She looks like my mother.
A man licks her neck.
It is hard to breathe with the world so thick,
my belly lowers to the ground.

On all fours, I cower around the Square.
With the thought of the food truck, I swell, fall
into line. Never before have I been obedient.

It goes on all night.
The day comes up—yellow light.
My eyes film over, my large back
can't tell if it's raining or not.

The air motored by odd desire,
the buttertruck idling on, I start to click
a beat of teeth, use my body for noise now.
I root and charge with vocal chords.
My lips drip with pigfoam, I spring a hiss,
burp with boundless offal breath on
everyone I pass. I fart my ass out,

bite buildings,
bite into piles of brick,
bite rodents apart.
I bite the thick air.
I bite at nothing.
I lick the savage ground.

My mother is ash in the ground.

The soldier in the truck likes my brown hair,
gives me a saucer of melted butter.
A hatchet in the corner.
I lick the butter,
grease over my teeth, he feeds
me dough, runs his hand down my spine,
no one has touched me in a long time,
flour, butter, sugar kneaded together.

In the confines of the food truck, my
breasts grow. From my full small chest,
fur falls. I touch my breasts to find their shape,
my face, soap wearing down.
I place my hand on my cunt.
The soldier turns to teasing, tells me to wet my sex,
then shuts butter, dough, and sugar away,
fastens close the truck's cupboards.
I buzz into the motor.

All the force of my mouth cups me
to the soldier. For dough, for motor, for mouth,
for running water. For melting butter.

For tooth against tooth, for tongue against tooth.
For breath, for mouth.
For bulletfear, for buildings flaking
away to dust. For motherash.
For love of father.
Want of mouth,
fear of words. For lisp and sing and suckle.
For mutter and mumble.
For bite.
For murmur.
For stuttering into the flakefilled sky.
For sugar water.
For every hiss and click
and sound that sinks through the dirt
and bombards the earth's core.
For cunt, for kick, for stumble.
For brother and sister.
For whisper, for kiss.

For passage and portal and entry inside.
Orifice. Rivermouth.
Water.

For exit and puke and spout and sluice.
For talkee-talkee and blah-blah-blah.

The soldier sings and I dream,
soothes himself singing
*sweetheart, high reeds, vineyards.*

My breasts tune to his sound,
my throat thirsts for wine from kegs.
Walls of his winecellar lined, thirst
of mine gone down to his groin.
I sprawl on the truck floor, asleep.

I wake screaming "Skin"
pointing to my fur, my pelt, my face.
The soldier rubs semen on my cheeks.

The truck revs up, plows through flocks
of crows, the driver's notes grow in pitch,
the black dots vanish.

On the road to Jasna Gora, we pass
pilgrims who want to see the fleshy scars
on *The Black Madonna*'s cheek. They want to see
the painting weep. They reach in their paper bags
for gristly ham and cheese.

Away from Kazimierz, freshness on my face,
I cut through the dark air, it is nearly
liquorlike, it stings at my cheeks.
How large my lungs feel as I walk the streets,
dissect the night's little details. Sky-high
reeds fill a lake.

There is enough light left in the sky to see
shapes of grape clusters in the vineyard.

I walk the rows between the fruit, distracted
by arbors turned colorless by night.
There is sugar in the sky.

Meal.
Lullabye.
Colicky infancy. Grapes
split open from lateness of season.
I come to the cemetery.
My mother is not buried there. I turn
back up the rows through the vineyard.
Vines are tied to trellises.

A bird leads me to the woods,
my father's face stays with my mind.
The weather turns wettish, slow.
Sleepy, my eyes close.

My thighs doze, my thumbs drowse.
Smoldering takes place in my lungs.
I cough, hot from fever.
The sky goes away.
I want my father.
Farther in, I bump trees,
can't move my gummy limbs.

No breath in the trees,
no wind in my lungs,
the woods and my body become one.

Struck still, I lie in the leaves
so the woods won't flame, so the fire stays in.
Red glistens before my eyes.
Black plum.
The yellow of scissored light through poplar.

Long-bellied birds of the woods are afraid now.
Harmless snakes fear death in the pot.
The woods' fields and clearings are in ill health.
Some ferns brown up and curl away,
the air smells hot and fungal.

I begin to feel serene, dig
my body deep in the leaves.
In and out goes my breath, it
breaks loose from my chest.

Disease shakes open the land, slits apart fields,
heaps up sludge.
Disease levels any seedling
that dares show its head.
The sun lags its way around
the far side of the globe.
My muscles lax, my back diffuse,
I lie in the leaves and look at my hands.
When finally, I rise up, begin to walk,
I am twisted and curved, a hunchback.

Breathing in the spring air stench,
I begin to paint.
I paint leaves black,
hold a snake with my hands and paint its back.

When menstrual blood begins to flow,
my thighs, my belly, my face
all become my canvas.

I build a chair,
the frame, thin branch, the seat from fur.
For three days straight, I stare at my feet,
think to paint my toes, but don't.
Cold comes up from the ground through my calves,
my lashes freeze, flakes are falling down.

A man leads the funeral on,
wears no clothes, snow falls,
his clarinet squawls.

A bony woman moves her bow back and forth,
her body angles, her chin sharp.
They bend a doyna inside out.

One man sings a love song from Lodz.
He sings low and looks down.
Snow builds on the back of his neck.
I begin to drum.
Men carry vessels of ash.
Girls carry baskets of violets and grass.

A man whose frame is large, whose skin falls
in folds, has a shovel strapped across his back.
With force, he sings.

The clarinetist slides notes around,
the mourners roll forward,
come to a pine that is black.

The large-framed man takes the shovel from his back.
We each enlarge the hole.
He digs extra long for those not there.

The violinist strays off, digs a cove,
lays in her violin.
She stretches out, does not get up.

From hunger, a girl chews violets.
Both singers sing no matter what.
A naked woman hides herself with grass.

I make a fire with wood from the pine,
smear ash on the drum,
spit on its head,
put the drum down,

head toward a clearing,
look back.

Klezmers slowly sing through the trees,
dressed in black rags,
all wearing hats.

*Yiz gad'al, ve yiz gad'ash,* all I know of kaddish.
*Yiz gad'al, ve yiz gad'ash,*

Stricken limbs,
stoned wind,
boned ground.

Mouth of wax.

A's, B's, C's, D's—fly
across the screen of sky

*Yiz gad'al*

When last I saw my mother's eyes
she squeezed them shut
Words could not open her face
her wide mute face

*ve yiz gad'ash*

# NOTES FOR "KAZIMIERZ SQUARE"

*schul*  The Yiddish word for a house of worship, commonly used for an orthodox synogogue.

*dahven (daven)*  To dahven is to pray. Dahvening suggests physically rocking back and forth while reciting the traditional liturgy.

*The Black Madonna*  The focus of Catholic worship in Poland is a painting called *The Black Madonna,* which depicts the Baby Jesus and the Virgin Mary with dark skin.

*Jasna Gora*  The church where *The Black Madonna* is enshrined.

*klezmers*  Jewish musicians from Eastern Europe who play music that is jazzlike or gypsylike in mood.

*doyna*  A smooth, improvised lament in the minor mode, usually played by a violin and clarinet.

*kaddish*  The Jewish prayer for the dead in which death is never mentioned.